Season of Rage

Season of Rage

Hugh Burnett and the
Struggle for Civil Rights

JOHN COOPER

Tundra Books

Published in Canada by Tundra Books,
481 University Avenue, Toronto, Ontario M5G 2E9

Published in the United States by Tundra Books of Northern New York,
P.O. Box 1030, Plattsburgh, New York 12901

Library of Congress Control Number: 2004109566

Library and Archives Canada Cataloguing in Publication

Cooper, John, 1958-
Season of rage : Hugh Burnett and the struggle for civil rights / John Cooper.

ISBN 0-88776-700-1

1. National Unity Association–History–Juvenile literature.
2. Black Canadians–Civil rights–Ontario–History–Juvenile literature.
3. Dresden (Ont.)–Race relations–History–Juvenile literature.
4. Civil rights movements–Ontario–History–Juvenile literature.
5. Racism–Ontario–History–Juvenile literature. 6. Race
discrimination–Ontario–Dresden–History–Juvenile literature.
I. Title.

FC3099.D64Z7 2005   323.1196'0713   C2004-904143-6

We acknowledge the financial support of the Government of Canada through the
Book Publishing Industry Development Program (BPIDP) and that of the Government of
Ontario through the Ontario Media Development Corporation's Ontario Book Initiative.
We further acknowledge the support of the Canada Council for the Arts and the
Ontario Arts Council for our publishing program.

Design: Cindy Reichle

Printed and bound in Canada

1 2 3 4 5 6   10 09 08 07 06 05

Dedicated to the memory of my father, John Joseph Cooper.

And dedicated to the charter members of the National Unity Association,
whose fight for justice deserves to be remembered and celebrated
by future generations of Canadians.

Note:
The terms *African-Canadian* and *black* are used interchangeably in the
text. The terms *Negro* and *colored* appear in historical references, as these terms
were used extensively in the 1950s to refer to people of African origin.

Contents

Prologue: One Man's Story

Once, there was a southern Ontario town called Dresden. Of its couple of thousand people, a few hundred were African-Canadians. In theory, these black people had the same rights as every other citizen of the town. But theory is not reality, and the reality of life for black people in this small town was marked by unfair treatment and the denial of many of those rights.

Beginning in 1943, one man made up his mind to change the way black people in his town were treated. Hugh Burnett was a twenty-four-year-old carpenter, but he had already been away from his hometown to take basic training as a soldier. World War II saw men and women – both black and white – fighting and getting killed in defense of liberty and democracy around the world. Hugh Burnett figured that if freedom was worth fighting for on the battlefields of Europe, then it was worth standing up for at home. So when the white owner of a restaurant refused to let him eat there – just because of the color of this skin – Burnett decided to make a stand.

More than half a century has passed since then, and many things have changed. Wars have been fought and brought to an end. Presidents and prime ministers have been elected and defeated. Children have grown up, gone to school, found jobs, been married, and had children of their own. Hugh Burnett's struggle against the prejudice he found in the town of Dresden might seem like no big deal. But history is made up of stories like his, little stories put together to become our shared story – our history. About the same time that Hugh

Burnett was trying to have the law changed in Dresden, Ontario, a black woman in Montgomery, Alabama, refused to give up her seat to a white man on a bus; four African-American college students sat down at a whites-only lunch counter in North Carolina; and nine black kids walked into an all-white high school in Little Rock, Arkansas.

Each of these stories may seem like no big deal. But taken together they make up an important part of the history of the civil-rights movement in North America, one of the most powerful and important stories of the 20th century.

Like all stories, it's hard to say when exactly it begins. Some people might say that Hugh Burnett's story began when his ancestors came to Canada to escape from slavery. Others might start the story even further back in time, when slavery was introduced to the North American colonies. Without doubt, the history of slavery helps to explain some of what happened later, not just in Dresden, but also in Alabama, North Carolina, Arkansas, and all the American states and Canadian provinces where black people now live.

Timeline: Up from Slavery

The journey from slavery to full equality was a long and difficult one. African-Americans, sometimes supported by white allies, had to fight for freedom. Even after they had won their freedom in legal terms, they had to fight for recognition of their rights as citizens. This timeline marks some of the significant stages of the journey leading to the beginning of the civil-rights movement in the 1950s and '60s.

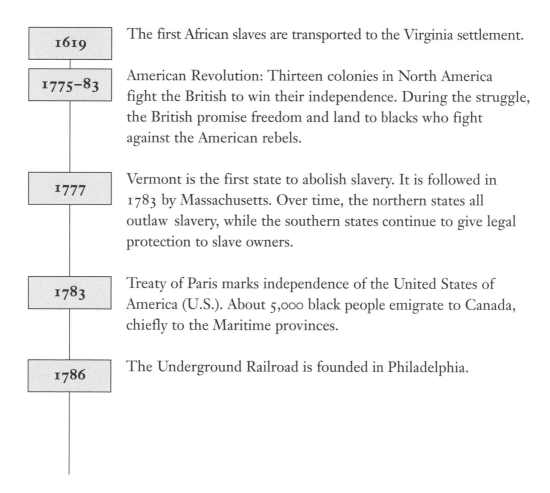

1619 — The first African slaves are transported to the Virginia settlement.

1775–83 — American Revolution: Thirteen colonies in North America fight the British to win their independence. During the struggle, the British promise freedom and land to blacks who fight against the American rebels.

1777 — Vermont is the first state to abolish slavery. It is followed in 1783 by Massachusetts. Over time, the northern states all outlaw slavery, while the southern states continue to give legal protection to slave owners.

1783 — Treaty of Paris marks independence of the United States of America (U.S.). About 5,000 black people emigrate to Canada, chiefly to the Maritime provinces.

1786 — The Underground Railroad is founded in Philadelphia.

The Underground Railway

A group of mainly white Quakers living in Philadelphia in the late 1700s were deeply opposed to slavery, and decided to help slaves escape from the South to the northern states where slavery was illegal. They called the escape route the Underground Railroad. It was not a real railroad, but a system of safe houses or "stations" where different people – "conductors" – would hide escaped slaves and show them the way to the next safe place on the route. Over the years, thousands of slaves made their way to freedom with the assistance of members of this dedicated secret organization.

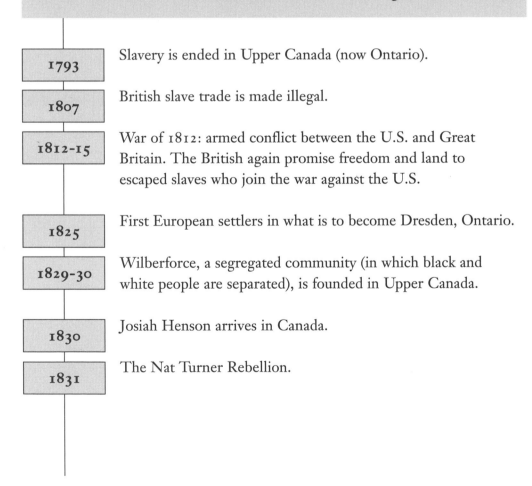

1793 Slavery is ended in Upper Canada (now Ontario).

1807 British slave trade is made illegal.

1812-15 War of 1812: armed conflict between the U.S. and Great Britain. The British again promise freedom and land to escaped slaves who join the war against the U.S.

1825 First European settlers in what is to become Dresden, Ontario.

1829-30 Wilberforce, a segregated community (in which black and white people are separated), is founded in Upper Canada.

1830 Josiah Henson arrives in Canada.

1831 The Nat Turner Rebellion.

MPI/Getty Images

A Bloody Uprising
Nat Turner, a slave, led more than sixty other slaves in Southampton County, Virginia, in revolt against their owners. Nearly sixty white people were killed. Turner was captured several weeks later and hanged.

| 1833 | Abolition Act makes slavery illegal in the British Empire, which includes Canada. |

| 1837 | First race riot in Canada leads to escape from jail of Solomon Moseby. |

The Moseby Incident

Slaves were not always safe when they arrived in Canada. Sometimes they were kidnapped and returned to their American owners. Although the Canadian government usually protected escaped slaves, the case of Solomon Moseby was an exception. Moseby stole a horse from his Kentucky owner in order to escape to Canada. When he crossed the border, he was arrested by the Niagara deputy sheriff and put in jail while the governor made up his mind what to do.

When they heard what had happened, members of the local African-Canadian community, led by their preacher Herbert Holmes, gathered around the jail to keep watch. When the governor gave the order to return Moseby to the U.S. – not because he was an escaped slave but because he stole a horse – there was a riot. Herbert Holmes and another black protester were killed by soldiers. Moseby escaped.

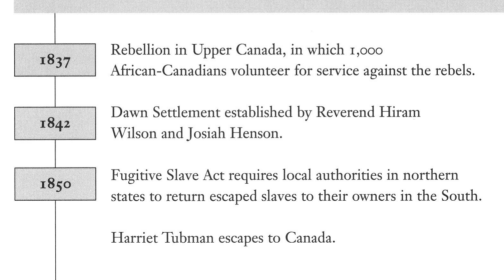

1837 Rebellion in Upper Canada, in which 1,000 African-Canadians volunteer for service against the rebels.

1842 Dawn Settlement established by Reverend Hiram Wilson and Josiah Henson.

1850 Fugitive Slave Act requires local authorities in northern states to return escaped slaves to their owners in the South.

Harriet Tubman escapes to Canada.

MPI/Getty Images

Harriet Tubman (1820–80)

I grew up like a neglected weed, – ignorant of liberty, having no experience of it. Then I was not happy or contented: every time I saw a white man I was afraid of being carried away. I had two sisters carried away in a chain-gang, – one of them left two children. We were always uneasy. Now I've been free, I know what a dreadful condition slavery is. I have seen hundreds of escaped slaves, but I never saw one who was willing to go back and be a slave. . . . I think slavery is the next thing to hell. If a person would send another into bondage, he would, it appears to me, be bad enough to send him into hell, if he could. – Harriet Tubman

Harriet Tubman was one of eleven children in a family born into slavery in Dorchester County, Maryland. When she was a girl, she was struck on the head by a weight thrown at her by a white overseer, and for the rest of her life she suffered from seizures and sometimes suddenly fell asleep. Just the same, she grew up with a strong body and an even stronger spirit.

She escaped from her owner in 1849 and lived for a while in Philadelphia. When the Fugitive Slave Act was passed in 1850, however, northern states no longer offered protection to escaped slaves. Tubman made her way to St. Catharines, in what is now Ontario, where she lived for a number of years.

But Tubman was not content to have achieved her own freedom. Between 1851 and 1857 she made repeated trips to the U.S. to rescue other slaves from their owners and lead them to freedom in Canada. She became so notorious for her exploits that a group of slave owners offered a bounty of $40,000 – an enormous sum for the time – for her capture "dead or alive." This didn't stop Tubman. She even returned to Maryland to rescue her parents. People called her "Moses," after the figure in the Christian Bible who led his people to the Promised Land.

| 1852 | Publication of *Uncle Tom's Cabin* by Harriet Beecher Stowe. |

| 1854 | Dresden, Ontario, is incorporated as a town. |

| 1857 | Dred Scott decision by the United States Supreme Court means that the American Constitution does not apply to slaves: a slave is still a slave even in a free state. |

| 1858 | John Brown tries to lead a black rebellion at Harper's Ferry, Virginia. The attempt fails and Brown is hanged in 1859. |

| 1860 | South Carolina legislature votes to secede from the Union, i.e., the United States. |

| 1861-65 | American Civil War. About 30,000 African-Canadians return to the U.S. to join more than 150,000 African-Americans who enlist in the Union Army. The northern Yankee states fight the breakaway southern Confederacy in a brutal war that ends in victory for the Union. |

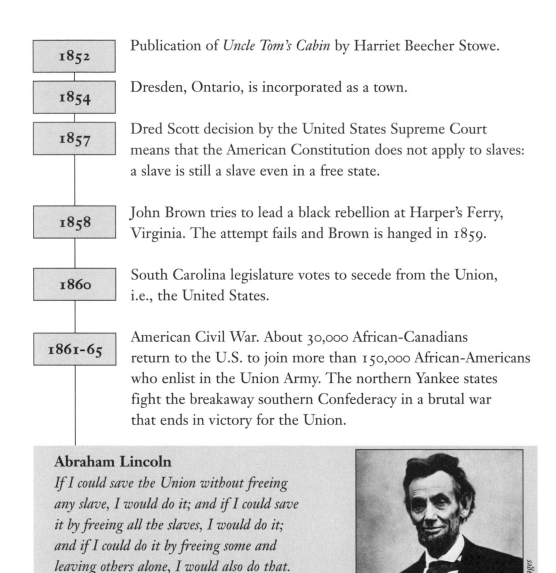

Abraham Lincoln

If I could save the Union without freeing any slave, I would do it; and if I could save it by freeing all the slaves, I would do it; and if I could do it by freeing some and leaving others alone, I would also do that.
– Abraham Lincoln

Getty Images

| 1863 | President Lincoln's Emancipation Proclamation declares slaves in the Confederate states to be free. |

| 1865-70 |

As many as half the escaped slaves who came to Canada before the Civil War return to the U.S.

| 1865 |

The Ku Klux Klan is founded.

Topical Press Agency/Getty Images

The Ku Klux Klan

The Invisible Empire of the Knights of the Ku Klux Klan (KKK) was founded in Pulaski, Tennessee, by a group of former Confederate soldiers. The organization recruited new members among white people who feared and resented the freedom given to black people by President Lincoln's Emancipation Proclamation.

Over the years, the KKK became established across the southern U.S. and in parts of Canada. Groups met at night wearing white robes and hoods that covered their faces. They set fire to wooden crosses as part of their strange ritual, and to scare and intimidate people. They physically attacked black people who insisted on their right to equal treatment under the law. Sometimes the KKK was guilty of murder. Because the white community, often including politicians and police officers, secretly supported them, KKK criminals and murderers were seldom brought to justice.

| 1896 | United States Supreme Court ruling in *Plessy v. Ferguson* makes separate public facilities for blacks and whites legal. |

Jim Crow

"Jim Crow" was the name invented by a white man pretending to be a black man in a "minstrel" show. Over time, the name came to describe the system in which black and white people were kept separate, or segregated.

In the southern U.S., the 1896 *Plessy v. Ferguson* ruling wiped out many of the gains made by black people after the Civil War. Railways and streetcars, public waiting rooms, restaurants, boarding houses, theaters, public parks, and swimming pools were segregated. Separate schools, hospitals, and other public institutions, generally of inferior quality, were set aside for black people.

Jim Crow laws remained in place until the 1950s and '60s, when the civil-rights movement challenged their legality.

| 1910 | National Association for the Advancement of Colored People (NAACP) is established "to promote equality of rights and eradicate caste or race prejudice." |

| 1910 | Canada Immigration Act allows federal officials to bar entry of "immigrants belonging to any race deemed unsuited to the climate requirements of Canada." The law is used to keep black people from entering Canada. |

Lynch Law

Southern whites prevented blacks from exercising their rights as free men and women in many ways. Some were subtle, some were obvious, and a few were violent. Nothing was more calculated to spread terror among the African-American population than "lynch law." From time to time, a white mob – often led by the KKK – would target a black man who had been accused, almost always falsely, of committing a crime against white people. They would seize, torture, and hang, or "lynch," him. Historian Harvard Sitkoff wrote,

Over a thousand were lynched between 1900 and 1915. No records exist to tally the number beaten or tortured. Nor can one describe adequately the terror of living with a constant fear of barbarity and violence, of having your security subject to the whim of those who despise you, of having no recourse to police or courts.

| 1930 | The Ku Klux Klan abducts Isabelle Jones (a white woman engaged to a black man) in Oakville, Ontario. |

| 1940-50 | Three-quarters of African-Americans in southern states are still denied the right to vote. |

| 1944 | Ontario Racial Discrimination Act makes it illegal to discriminate on the basis of race, color, or creed. |

| 1947 | Jack Roosevelt "Jackie" Robinson becomes the first black player to play on an integrated major-league baseball team. |

Allan Grant/ Time Life Pictures/ Getty Images

Major-League Hero

Black people have fought to break down the color barrier in many areas of life – including professional sports. Jackie Robinson challenged the prejudices of both team owners and fans when he became the first black player on a major-league baseball team – the Brooklyn Dodgers – in 1947. He possessed astonishing skills as a player, and was Rookie of the Year in his first season. In his third season, he was named the National League's Most Valuable Player, leading the League in hitting (with an average of .342) and stolen bases (37), while hitting 124 runs. Over the course of his ten years with the Dodgers, the team won six pennants. For a decade, Robinson dominated the game. But Robinson did as much off the field as on it to change people's attitudes towards black people. His quiet dignity and strong character commanded respect from everyone who encountered him.

Dresden's Early Years

Far from Canada's big cities, with their bustling crowds, department stores, factories, and offices, lies a little town called Dresden. Tucked away near the southwest corner of the province, it's far away from Ontario's capital of Toronto. It's far enough away from Windsor and Detroit that it doesn't have what we often think of as big-city worries, yet it's close enough for folks to pay a visit.

But don't make the mistake of calling it a sleepy little town because, ever since Europeans first settled there in 1825, the Dresden area has had a busy history. The tiny community was first called Fairport. Back then, lumber merchants and farmers from the British Isles, Germany, and the Netherlands thought it was a great place to put down roots, and they soon pushed out most of the original Aboriginal population, whose land was sold to the British government.

The land around what would become Dresden had rich, dark soil. A dense green carpet of trees – pine, maple, birch, oak, and more – stretched around the land, and bears, deer, foxes, and wolves wandered the forests. Birds sang throughout the day; rabbits raced across open fields. In the evening, bullfrogs croaked in ponds and swamps. For lumber merchants, the dense forests were filled with mature, 200-year-old trees perfect for building houses, tables, and the decks of ships for the British Navy. The Sydenham River wound its way through the land and made it easy to carry goods and people by boat.

The British colonial government encouraged the settlement of newcomers to the area, part of what was then known as Upper Canada West. The newcomers came in droves with tools and technology, and worked hard to cut great swaths through the forests. Once the land was cleared, farmers tilled it. Over time, the old stands of trees were replaced with fields of wheat, tomatoes, barley, corn, and beans. Farmers found the long growing season and plentiful rain to their liking.

Brightly colored homes sprang up on the land like wildflowers, rising up as if in celebration of a new time in the lives of the settlers and this new country. By the 1850s, the community had a store, a hotel, and a schoolhouse. In 1852 it had a post office, and with it came its new name: the village of Dresden, named for a town in Germany. Its birth date would be celebrated as 1854.

Farmers would travel into the village in horse-drawn wagons to trade their goods for new farm tools, food, and household goods. Here, they could get news from other parts of the country, as well as from Europe and the U.S. Just a few miles to the south, the town of Chatham was growing strongly, and would go on to become a major local center for trade and industry that would attract thousands of people. To the east, Toronto, Kingston, and Ottawa were the big cities where political decisions were made. In 1857 – ten years before Canada would become its own country – it was announced that Ottawa would be the nation's capital. But for those who made Dresden their home, the little village – just a few hundred strong – suited them, and they weren't interested in having their community get any bigger.

Dresden was also rich in the history of Canada and its people. It was one of the end points of the northward migration of slaves from the U.S. who sought freedom in Canada during the middle part of the 1800s, using a route called the Underground Railroad. Southwestern Ontario became known, not only as a place to settle in freedom, but also as a place where abolitionists (those who wanted to bring an end to slavery) made plans to assist in the slaves' escape.

Many of the slaves who came north to freedom settled in the Dresden area. In 1840, a group of escaped slaves, abolitionists, and Quakers purchased more than 200 acres of land on the Sydenham River near Dresden. There the group founded the Dawn Settlement, a colony made up of farmers and workers who ran a sawmill and a brickyard. The community grew to more than 500 residents who worked and traded with people in the surrounding area. Along with other farming communities, the Dawn Settlement helped to establish African-Canadians as important contributors to Canadian society and its economic development. The Dawn Settlement lasted for thirty years. It became the backbone of southwestern Ontario's African-Canadian community, and many of the families that live in the area today got their start at the Dawn Settlement.

Courtesy of Uncle Tom's Cabin Museum, Dresden

Josiah Henson (1789–1883)

It was the 28th of October, 1830, in the morning, when my feet first touched the Canada shore. I threw myself on the ground, rolled in the sand, seized handfuls of it and kissed them, and danced around, til, in the eyes of several who were present, I passed for a madman. – Josiah Henson

Josiah Henson was born a slave in Charles County, Maryland. When he was a young man, a white overseer struck him so hard on the back with a piece of wood that Henson's shoulders were broken, and he was maimed for life. Still, he served his owner faithfully for many years, and gained the man's trust. He had Henson lead a group of slaves on a journey that took them to the banks of the Ohio River, where they could have easily crossed and escaped to freedom, but Henson insisted upon completing his mission.

Henson's owner promised that he would set him free one day. Instead, he tried to sell him "down the river" to a Southern plantation owner and into a much harder life. When he understood that he had been betrayed, Henson made his escape and, at the age of forty-one, settled in Canada.

Henson was one of the founders of the Dawn Settlement. With support from the British Anti-Slavery Society, he established the British American Institute, a school that provided former slaves with training in different trades, allowing them a good start in their new lives as free persons.

Henson became well-known when he put down the details of his life in a book, *The Life of Josiah Henson, Formerly a Slave, Now an Inhabitant of*

Canada, which was published in 1849. Another book published just three years later, *Uncle Tom's Cabin* by Harriet Beecher Stowe, achieved much greater success. Stowe's book was a novel about how horrible life was for slaves, how they yearned for freedom, and how some escaped by way of the Underground Railroad. More than 300,000 copies of Stowe's novel were sold in the first year after it was published. It inspired many people to make a stand against slavery.

There were similarities between Henson's real life and the imagined life of Uncle Tom in Stowe's novel. Many people came to believe that Henson was, in fact, the model for the novel's title character. Whether or not this is true, Henson was a famous member of the Canadian black community, and a powerful symbol for the abolitionist movement in the United States. He died in Dresden in 1883.

The whole Dresden area has a history built on the diligence and ingenuity of black pioneers who created lives for themselves in Canada, first in settlements like Dawn and nearby Buxton, and then in the surrounding community. Those early African-Canadian pioneers built many of the schools and churches in the area, some of which still stand today.

By the early 1900s, roads were beginning to be paved, connecting the town to other towns and cities. There was a railroad to carry carloads of goods. The Sydenham River carried boatloads of people and goods; when the water was low, tow ropes were used to pull the boats over the river's shallow spots. The town itself became known for careful craftsmanship and the detailed and beautiful architecture of its homes, schools, and churches. People lived by the seasons: tilling and planting in the spring, maintaining their farms over the hot summer, harvesting their vegetables in the fall, and perhaps finding work at a local factory during the winter. Throughout the year, they would find warm, welcoming, and friendly faces on the town's two major thoroughfares, Main Street and St. George Street. It was a pleasant place, where people could perhaps buy a farm or run a business, find work, raise a family, and live a productive life.

Racism – Anger, Fear, Hatred

Old attitudes are difficult to overcome. For many years, members of the white community treated blacks with little or no respect. Their attitudes were born hundreds of years before, and were often ingrained in the culture of white people whose ancestors came to North America from Europe.

The terrible attitudes focused on the wrongheaded notion that black people were inferior to white people, less intelligent and less capable of doing good work. Ideas like this created a system by which, long after the end of the Civil War in the U.S., white people prevented black people from having any chance to receive a good education or a decent job. Too often, blacks weren't able to eat in the same restaurants as white people, use the same public washrooms, drink from the same water fountains, or even walk on the same side of the street. These attitudes were also prevalent in Canada where, despite promises of freedom, blacks were still treated as second-class citizens. In many places in both Canada and the U.S., you could find successful black people who created a good life and wealth for themselves, in spite of the obstacles placed in their way. But for most, it was a very difficult life.

All over Canada, racism was a fact of life. And racist attitudes would, in some cases, either become the law or be reinforced by the laws of the land. In some towns and cities in Canada, black children were made to go to separate schools from whites, even as recently as the 1960s. In other places, if you were white and you didn't want to sell your house to a black person, you could legally spell that out in the sales agreement. If you were a black person and wanted to eat in a restaurant, the owner could refuse to serve you and get away with it. If you were a white storekeeper, you could refuse to serve a black customer and no one would question you about your actions. As a black person, you might be expected to address white people as "Sir" or "Madam" at all times.

In schools, black kids would be called racist names or be challenged to fights. As adults, black citizens were often denied bank loans for no good reason. If they could get insurance, they were charged higher premiums than those that white people paid. For a majority of black people, there were very few jobs, except as janitors or maids, or as porters serving passengers on the railroad. And in social situations, African-Canadians might be called derogatory names, from "colored" and "Negro" to the shameful and hate-filled "nigra" and "nigger."

The Klan in Oakville

On a Friday night in February 1930, members of the KKK, dressed in their white robes and hoods, set fire to a wooden cross on one of the main streets in Oakville, Ontario. Hundreds of townspeople stood by and did nothing. The dozens of Klansmen then made their way to the house where a black man, Ira Johnson, was staying with his fiancée, a white woman named Isabelle Jones. Johnson, a veteran of World War I, was well-known in Oakville's black community. But the KKK would not hear of a black man getting married to a white woman. They seized Isabelle Jones and drove her to Hamilton, Ontario, where her mother lived. They were stopped on the way by Oakville's chief of police who, amazingly, did nothing to interfere with their actions.

It was only after complaints were made by black and Jewish organizations in Toronto that some of the people involved in the Oakville incident were brought to trial. Three men were charged, not with abduction or disturbing the peace, but with "wearing a disguise without lawful excuse." The police chief testified that the Klan leader, a Hamilton man, was someone he "knew quite well." In explaining why he did nothing, he told a reporter: "There was no semblance of disorder and the visitors' [meaning the Klan's] behavior was all that could be desired."

The chief culprit in the raid was found guilty, fined $50, and later imprisoned for three months. But the incident showed clearly that the sympathy of many white people in Oakville was with the Klan, not with the Klan's victims.

Racist attitudes were reflected in rules that prevented equal treatment in public places. At Rondeau Park not far from Dresden, for example, blacks were not allowed to use the change rooms to get into their swimsuits. In Amherstburg, near Windsor and the border with the U.S., there were laws that prohibited black people from being on the streets after ten o'clock at night.

Similarly, blacks were unwelcome in many stores, restaurants, and movie theaters. Throughout Ontario, and especially in southwestern Ontario, white-owned businesses would hang signs in their windows that said "No Coloreds Allowed." In Chatham, blacks would not be served in the coffee shop of the William Pitt Hotel. And often they found their way barred when they tried to find employment or a place to live.

In many cities, discrimination – when you openly or privately prevent people from enjoying the same rights as you do – was extended to other groups as well, such as Jewish, Italian, Chinese, and Japanese people. If you were a black high-school or university student in Windsor, you knew it was a waste of time to apply to the Chrysler automotive plant for a summer job: there was an unwritten policy against hiring "coloreds." Some of those attitudes were enshrined in local laws. In 1948, the country's highest court, the Supreme Court of Canada, upheld a local law in the community of Grand Bend, Ontario, that forbade "Jews and Negroes" from owning property.

In Dresden, black kids would hang out with white kids, but only at the hockey arena, the swimming hole, or the baseball diamond. Two of Dresden's three restaurants, Kay's Café and Emerson's Soda Bar Restaurant, would not serve black customers. All of the city's five barbershops and its one beauty parlor refused service to African-Canadians, as did the three pool halls.

In 1954, Dresden's St. George Street was typical of most small-town main streets, with a drug store, restaurants, barbershops, and gas stations. What wasn't typical was the discrimination that took place in many of those businesses. Courtesy of the Dresden Branch of the Chatham-Kent Public Library

As an African-Canadian, you just knew that in Dresden, across Ontario, and in the rest of Canada there were places – clubs, stores, restaurants, churches, and schools – where you were not welcome. It was as simple, and as complicated, as that.

It didn't make sense. Black Canadians paid their taxes, contributed to their communities, and knew they were entitled to the same treatment as everyone else. Several African-Canadians, faced with discrimination, took their fight to the local government. Other blacks who suffered discrimination hired lawyers and fought in court against unfair treatment, but they often lost.

In 1945 in Toronto, a young black man named Harry Gairey, Jr., tried to go skating at his local skating rink, the Icelandia. He was told to leave because of his skin color. His father, Harry Gairey, Sr., took the case to his local alderman, Joe Salsberg. After all, Gairey reasoned, the Ontario government had passed a law, the Ontario Racial Discrimination Act, just a year before. The Ontario premier had made a clear connection between the war that Canadians were fighting overseas and the importance of freedom and equality at home. "If you discriminate against any person because of race or creed in respect to their rights as a citizen," Premier Drew had said, "you deny that equality which is part and parcel of the very freedom we are fighting to preserve."

The problem? Few people cared about the Racial Discrimination Act, and the police had no interest in enforcing it. But Joe Salsberg and the Jewish community, itself the target of many acts of discrimination, began pushing Toronto City Council for changes that would eventually lead to laws outlawing discrimination.

Gairey was looking for justice. But justice wouldn't come easily. It wouldn't simply be handed to African-Canadians. It had to be demanded, even wrenched from the hands of an unwilling society.

So many white Americans and Canadians signed up to serve in the armed forces during World War II that a huge number of jobs became available for black people. Many black men and women found work in factories that had been closed to them before. They were able to learn trades and to move into more highly paid jobs. After the war was over, economic growth surged – business and industry grew. More people came from Europe, Asia, and the West Indies to find jobs in Canadian cities. Schools and universities expanded to give men and women returning from the war the training they needed now that the war was over. Increasingly, activists were pushing for the civil rights that had long been denied to black people in the U.S.

Change was in the air. Across the North American continent, black people began to believe that the long period of discrimination and oppression might come to an end. Even among some white people, there was recognition that the words used to justify the war – words like "freedom" and "democracy" – would have no meaning unless the legitimate claims of black people were recognized.

Hugh Burnett

Every Sunday, Hugh Burnett attended services with his family at the Union Baptist Church in Dresden. After church, Hugh and his younger brother Gordon would often take a walk along the quiet streets of town. One Sunday in 1931, when Hugh was twelve years old, he and Gordon went to a local Chinese restaurant.

It was an especially warm summer afternoon. A gentle breeze caused the cornstalks in the surrounding fields to sway like thousands of emerald green dancers moving together in time to an unheard rhythm. The air held the hint of a coming storm. The occasional tractor puttered down St. George Street, which ran through the center of town, past the IGA grocery store, the Rexall drugstore, and the Texaco gas station. A few cars huffed and puffed down the street. Horses snorted as they pulled their owners' buggies, heading for home and the promise of a snack of oats in the stable. The only places open in a town dotted with Christian churches were the restaurants and the local dairy bar.

Hugh, who already possessed the lean and wiry frame that he would carry into adulthood, asked the proprietor of the Chinese restaurant for ice cream for himself and Gordon. At first they were thinking of cones, but the two brothers decided they had enough time to sit down and eat their treat from a dish. A few customers were seated at tables in the restaurant, but not all of the tables were occupied. The owner knew both boys well, had known them all their lives, and was pleased to sell them the ice cream. But then he leaned over the counter and told them that they would have to eat it in the kitchen.

Hugh said he didn't understand. The owner offered no explanation. Hugh and Gordon left the restaurant without the ice cream.

To say that the incident made Hugh angry would be an understatement. He realized that he and Gordon had been treated this way only because of their skin color. His previous life of accepting others, and being accepted by them, had changed. Hugh made up his mind, then and there, to fight against discrimination.

Myrtle and Robert Burnett on their wedding day. Descendants of slaves who escaped to Canada via the Underground Railroad, they owned a farm just outside of Dresden. Courtesy of Gordon Burnette

Hugh's father Robert Burnett was a mix of African-Canadian and First Nation Cherokee whose family came to Canada from the southern U.S. in the 1800s. It was common at the beginning of the 20th century for African-Canadians to marry Aboriginal people, especially in southwestern Ontario, and many families who have homes and farms in the Dresden area proudly count blacks and Natives among their ancestors.

Myrtle Carter's family arrived in Canada in the 1850s and settled in Raleigh Township. Myrtle was one of ten children. Her parents, Sarah Jones Carter and George Elbert Carter, owned a farm and were members of the local Baptist Church. George was also the secretary-treasurer of the local school.

Robert and Myrtle were married and settled down on a farm a few kilometers outside Dresden to raise a family. Their children worked alongside them – raising their farm animals and working on the family's crop of vegetables, wheat, and oats – before heading off to school.

Hugh was born in 1919. When he was twenty, he was called up for military service and took basic training, but was discharged after only a couple of months because of a stomach problem. He went back to work on the farm and, in 1941, married his longtime girlfriend Beatrice.

Although Beatrice and Hugh Burnett both were born and grew up in the Dresden area, after their wedding they lived for a few years in Windsor, Ontario. Courtesy of the Burnett family

Hugh and Beatrice moved to Windsor, just across the border from Detroit, Michigan, where Hugh worked for the Ford Motor Company for several years. In 1948, they moved back to Dresden, bought some property, and built their own home. Hugh began using his carpentry skills around Dresden, building houses and cabinets for his neighbors. Tall and strong, he was a good person to work with on a job site. Many of his shorter co-workers would say with a chuckle that he was "better than a stepladder!" And it was said, too, that nobody could build a finer cabinet than Hugh Burnett.

Around this time, Hugh began spelling his name with an "e" on the end – as *Burnette* – because some white people in town were mispronouncing his name. They were saying it as "Burn-it" instead of properly pronouncing it as "Bur-net." With its echoes of the actions of the KKK and its cross-burnings, it offended Hugh, who had never forgotten his early encounter with racial discrimination in the town.

Although tall, Hugh was not a big man, and his voice, like that of his father, Robert, was mild and soft-spoken. But there was a ribbon of steel that ran through him, and a keen edge of spiritual strength in his decision to challenge the attitudes of the day. The fires of that decision would continue to burn for more than twenty-five years. This came as no surprise to his family. They knew that when Hugh made up his mind to do something, he could not be swayed from following through on his chosen path.

The National Unity Association

Dresden was a long way from Canada's capital city, Ottawa. And those whose minds were occupied with earning a living from the land may not have spared much thought about law and justice. But in 1943, Hugh Burnett sent a letter to the federal government in Ottawa complaining about racial discrimination at Kay's Café. The owner, Morley McKay, was well-known for his obstinate refusal to serve black patrons. The government took no action.

In 1948, Hugh launched a lawsuit against McKay. But figuring he might lose, as others had in the past, he soon gave up on it. One thing he did recognize was that he needed to take action not as an individual, but as part of a group. The power of numbers would be the only way to make sure that change would happen in the town. He was tired of the hatred and discrimination, and knew it had to end.

Hugh didn't have to look far for support, because other blacks who lived in and around Dresden had the same idea. In 1948, Hugh joined with several others to form the National Unity Association, or NUA. And it made sense that one of the key co-founders of the NUA would be Hugh's boyhood friend Alvin Ladd.

You couldn't find a pair of friends who appeared to be more different. Hugh Burnett was a lean, quiet thinker, while Alvin had the strong, muscled build of someone who used his strength to earn his living. Alvin was born in 1920, just a year after Hugh, and the pair had grown up together, living on farms just over

More than 50 years after helping form the National Unity Association, Alvin Ladd is the last surviving charter member. John Cooper

a mile apart. Alvin shared Hugh's concern over the treatment of African-Canadians. He had grown up facing discrimination in Dresden and other towns and, like others in the black community, had been forced to accept the poor treatment he received. But he knew it wasn't right. This became especially clear after he served in the Canadian military from 1942 to 1946. He recognized that serving your country during a war should entitle you to better treatment during peaceful times. After his military service ended, Alvin worked as a truck driver with the City of Chatham, a job he held until he retired.

The NUA's first meeting took place in the modest farmhouse of Hugh's uncle, Bernard Carter, just outside of Dresden. The organization's founding members included Arthur Alexander, Percy Carter, Joseph Hanson, Lorne Ladd, Leroy Poole, Frank Richardson, Fred Robinson, and Philip Shadd. Shadd, a farmer, was spokesperson for the group – and an impressive figure as well, with hands that were described as "twice the size of a normal man's hands, gigantic, tough and strong, and more than fit for the hard work of a farmer." Like Shadd, most of the NUA's founders were farmers or tradespeople who did a lot of business with Dresden's white community. They were honest, fair people who had simply had enough of the shoddy treatment of the past.

The fire for justice that burned in Hugh Burnett was ignited inside each member of the group, as they sat in Bernie Carter's living room and laid out their plans to challenge the system. They took their message to others in the community, and soon the NUA grew to more than a hundred members, all drawn from Dresden and the surrounding farms and towns.

The association needed the support of as many citizens, associations, and politicians outside its own community as possible, so letter-writing became a major occupation for the group. They would meet at members' homes and discuss who should receive letters and how the group should approach the subject. The NUA's simple motto appeared at the top of the hundreds of letters written by Hugh Burnett: *Organized in the interest of better race and group relations.*

Before the town's civic election in the autumn of 1948, the National Unity Association went to Dresden's municipal offices. Its members wanted to address the town council and get their grievances out in the open.

The group asked the all-white Dresden Town Council, under the leadership of Mayor William Weese, to ensure that a policy of non-discrimination was in place before it would issue licenses to local businesses. In other words, the NUA asked that licenses be granted only to those businesspeople who agreed not to discriminate. Hugh pointed out to the council that other towns already had non-discrimination bylaws in place. Only one Dresden council member, Michael Fry, was in favor of the NUA's proposal. Otherwise, the representatives of the town of Dresden were unmoved. The group left the municipal building in defeat.

While some townspeople were also in favor of the NUA's motion, most just didn't care. They believed that the problem would go away if they just left it alone. The town council truly represented Dresden's citizens – and those citizens wanted to go about their own business, tend to their gardens, sweep their porches, cut their lawns, and visit with friends. The last thing they wanted was to draw attention to a situation that made them uncomfortable. They thought Hugh and his group were troublemakers who were trying stir up anger and resentment in the town's African-Canadian population.

At the same time, some African-Canadian families also wanted to continue lying low. It was understandable – the Ku Klux Klan was still known to be active in parts of Canada, and there was a chance that African-Canadian businesses and way of life could be damaged if attention were drawn to the town's racial problems. But the NUA pressed on.

Not long after the council meeting, Councillor Fry received a death threat from an anonymous phone caller. Hugh and his uncle Bill Carter received a death threat, too, in a note marked with a skull-and-crossbones. Part of the letter read,

> *Go easy Mr. Carter, or you and Hugh Burnette will be destroyed. Bring on your riots. We are ready for you . . . We will fix you quick and don't forget to come.*

The NUA Finds an Ally

A short time after the NUA's defeat by the Dresden Town Council, Hugh looked outside the community for support. The NUA called on the Jewish Labour Committee, an organization that was fighting for the rights of workers in business and industry across Canada. The Jewish Labour Committee was led by Kalmen Kaplansky, a veteran of World War II who had been fighting against anti-Semitism and for the rights of workers for years. The committee had ties to the Toronto Association for Civil Liberties, which was involved in pushing for better treatment of people everywhere. In 1949, the two groups formed the Committee on Group Relations.

That same year, after hearing Hugh Burnett's story, and with a mission to address Canada's social inequities, the Committee on Group Relations went to the Ontario government. Their mission took them to the Ontario Legislature, an imposing building of pink sandstone located in Toronto, the province's capital. There they met Premier Frost himself.

Leslie Frost became premier of Ontario in April 1949, and ran the province for twelve years. His success was based on shrewd thinking and his ability to bring people together and forge a compromise. What set Frost apart from other politicians was his willingness – for his principles – to go against the tide of human feeling. Born and raised in the town of Orillia, he would become known in the province as "Old Man Ontario" for his commitment to what he called his "small-town" approach to politics.

He was a tall, strongly built man with a mantle of graying hair pushed back to reveal a high forehead. With his spectacles perched on his nose, and turned out in the finest tailored suits of the day, Frost was the picture of an intelligent, highly educated lawyer and politician. When meeting people, he would grip their hand strongly with his own, put his free hand on their arm or shoulder, and begin telling them why his small-town values were important in moving the province forward into the future.

The delegation that entered Frost's office that day in 1949 consisted of thirty-six human-rights activists representing more than sixty-two different organizations. They asked the Ontario government for a law to ensure that any person who went for a job interview would be treated fairly. In keeping with the NUA's request to Dresden's town council the previous year, the delegation also asked that the province create a law to force municipalities to cancel the licenses of businesses that discriminated against their customers.

Premier Frost appeared to welcome their proposals, but he did not act immediately to answer the NUA's concerns. He was worried that he would need more time to convince his cabinet ministers that change was needed. Many of them were narrow-minded and wanted to believe that discrimination was nothing but the product of some people's imaginations.

Back in Dresden, the town council still insisted on having things its way. It agreed to hold a referendum, or public vote, on the discrimination issue in December 1949. The referendum asked citizens to vote on whether businesses should be given a license if they planned to discriminate against customers. Overwhelmingly, by a vote of almost four to one, Dresden residents came out in favor of discrimination. In Dresden, shops and restaurants providing services to the public could continue to turn away African-Canadian customers.

This disappointing result led the Toronto Association for Civil Liberties to ask for another meeting with Premier Frost. In January 1950, the Association, this time representing 104 organizations including the NUA, brought a delegation of more than 800 people to the provincial government at Queen's Park.

There, the group told Premier Frost that the Dresden situation was proof that the province of Ontario needed not one, but two new laws. The first, which had already been agreed to, would be enacted into law as the Fair Employment

Ontario Premier Leslie Frost (seated, center) with his Cabinet in 1949. Archives of Ontario

Practices Act. It would guarantee that individuals could not be discriminated against when applying for a job. But the delegation now asked for a second law that would prevent discrimination in places like restaurants.

In their brief – a written document – to the premier, the group asked for better legislation to protect individuals from the effect of racism. It said that, since its first request six months earlier, the situation in Dresden had gotten worse, and it was time for legislation that would "combat discrimination in employment, housing, and public places, in the form of a Fair Employment Practices Act and amendments to the Ontario Racial Discrimination Act."

"A Brief to the Ontario Premier" pointed out that the group was not introducing radically new ideas, but rather principles that were already accepted by the government when it sponsored the Ontario Racial Discrimination Act in 1944.

As he had at the previous meeting, Premier Frost responded positively to the presentation. He knew that fairness was in line with better economic development. As premier, he wanted more people to come to the province to build the industries needed to give people more jobs, a better education, and a good life. If white people were allowed to continue discriminating against African-Canadians, Italians, Portuguese, Chinese, people from the West Indies, and others, it would hurt the economy.

Although Frost supported the delegation's demands, other members of his government resisted the changes they asked for. The politicians at Queen's Park didn't want to upset their constituents, and many of the voters remained prejudiced. It would be some time before Frost could convince his colleagues of the need for change.

In 1951, the government passed Canada's first Fair Employment Practices Act. The Act stated that it was "contrary to public policy" to discriminate "on the basis of race, creed, colour, nationality, ancestry or place of origin" when hiring people in a workplace. The premier followed this with a law intended to ensure that women, who were often paid less than men, were paid fairly: the Female Employees Fair Remuneration Act. But no action was taken to prohibit discrimination in restaurants and stores.

The Protest Grows

Through 1952, the NUA continued to maintain contact with activists in Toronto, and was active in protesting discrimination in its community. It challenged a local civic organization, the Dresden Rebecca Lodge, and its use of a "black face" or "minstrel" show. "Black face" originated in the 1800s and was considered an insult to blacks. These shows involved white actors wearing dark makeup and making fun of the stereotyped behavior of blacks – their singing, dancing, and acting silly was a parody of how it was believed black people behaved. For the NUA, the show reinforced outdated white attitudes.

In a letter to the Dresden Rebecca Lodge, Hugh Burnett wrote, "We sincerely hope that you will accept this note constructively. We are not trying to force you to cancel your show. Our aim is to point out the fact that such a show does not lend any support to better race relations."

Hugh's easygoing manner, tempered by a strong desire to be heard and understood, made him an effective spokesperson for the NUA. Along with fellow NUA founder Philip Shadd, he spoke often to the news media. And while the local *Chatham Daily News* did not pay much attention to the group's activities, it seemed that the farther you got from the town of Dresden, the greater the interest in the issue of discrimination. From the *Windsor Star*, *London Free Press*, *Toronto Star*, *Toronto Telegram*, and *Globe and Mail*, the NUA received an increasing amount of newspaper coverage.

By 1953, Hugh Burnett was busy working and raising a family with Beatrice. His carpentry business was doing well. His advertisements in the local newspapers proclaimed, "No job too large or too small . . . 20 Years Experience." Few in the community could lay down a better plan, saw a straighter board, or hammer a nail with as much skill or authority. With a team of skilled craftsmen – both black and white – working for him, he could raise the roof of a house in a short time, creating snug family homes that still stand today. People appreciated him for his skills and, while he was quiet and thoughtful, he carried himself with the strength of character that clearly let people know he was a good person to have around. And Hugh would carry his sense of justice with him always. It was as much a part of his equipment as his tool belt, tape measure, carpenter's level, and T-square were.

In the early 1950s, Hugh Burnett's truck was often seen around Dresden, proof of his prosperous carpentry business. Courtesy of the Burnett family

Like Hugh, the town had changed over the years – at least outwardly. The downtown was still quaint and old-fashioned. The post office at the corner of Main and St. George still dominated the business district, just as it had in Hugh's youth. But more stores crowded along the streets, and brightly lit signs sprang up here and there. By the early 1950s, horse-drawn wagons and antique cars were replaced by the flatbed and pickup trucks being turned out by the factories of Windsor and Detroit, just down the highway. Big cars made by Ford and General Motors – massive vehicles made of steel and chrome – roared down the length of St. George Street. More roads crisscrossed the countryside around the town every year, taking Dresden's citizens on trips that led to bigger places and brought them into contact with new people and fresh ideas.

There was as much talk at mid-century about space exploration as there was about fighting the Communists. Television sets were beginning to appear in people's homes, and television programming was starting to move ahead of radio in popularity. The newspaper business was highly competitive, as different newspapers fought to be the one paper every citizen had to read – the so-called "newspaper war" in Toronto was especially intense.

But old ideas refused to die. Hugh and the NUA continued to push the government to address their concerns in Dresden. The province's attorney general (the person responsible for Ontario's laws) told Hugh there was no legal power to prohibit racial discrimination in places like Dresden, where local businesses continued to turn their backs on black patrons.

Hugh wrote to Donna Hill, who was the secretary of the Toronto and District Joint Labour Committee to Combat Racial Intolerance – sometimes referred to as the Joint Labour Committee for Human Rights, and eventually as just the Joint Labour Committee. The Committee was located in a tiny office in a small, red-brick building on Spadina Road in Toronto. Donna, who was white, and her husband Daniel G. Hill, who was black, were very active in Canada's civil-rights movement. After marrying in Washington, D.C., in 1953, they moved to Canada, where they assumed their marriage would be better received. This wasn't necessarily the case, but at least in Canada – unlike some places in the U.S. – they could not be convicted under the law for having an interracial marriage.

Daniel and Donna Hill in 1954, not long after they moved to Canada. Donna was instrumental in helping the National Unity Association begin its challenge of racist attitudes in Dresden. Daniel Hill would go on to lead Ontario's first Human Rights Commission. Courtesy of Donna Hill

Donna Hill knew the issues of racism well; she had attended an integrated college (one that accepted both white and black students) in the U.S., and at one time had worked with a civil-rights organization in Ohio. She also volunteered for the Congress on Racial Equality (CORE), where her work included civil-rights sit-in demonstrations at segregated drugstores that refused to serve black customers.

While its offices were small, the Joint Labour Committee was supported by large and important labor organizations. Its board members were some of the most respected civil-rights activists in the country. Bromley Armstrong and Dennis McDermott were active in the labor movement, and Stanley Grizzle, working as a union representative with the Brotherhood of Sleeping Car Porters, had helped bring a union to Canada to ensure that black railroad porters were given fair treatment in the workplace. The Joint Labour Committee had been active in challenging attitudes in the workplace and in rental accommodations for several years. Earlier, the committee had challenged the practice of discrimination at the William Pitt Hotel in Chatham, where blacks were being refused service.

One day in late 1953, Donna Hill met with Hugh Burnett, Philip Shadd, and Bernie Carter in her office in Toronto. The three men sat down and poured out to her the saga of their struggle to end racial discrimination in Dresden. Hill was shocked, but not surprised. It confirmed what she and the committee had already seen: Canadians were not only refusing to do anything about discrimination, they were refusing to acknowledge that it existed. She began setting a course of action for the Joint Labour Committee to work with the NUA.

Through the early months of 1954, Hugh Burnett and the National Unity Association, along with Donna Hill and Sid Blum (who would take over from Hill in June 1954, when she left to have a baby), gathered information about the conditions of life in Dresden. Like Donna Hill, Sid Blum was especially well-suited for his duties with the group. He was born in the U.S. and, as a Jew, had experienced anti-Semitism. Active in the civil-rights movement, he was unafraid to take on the challenges of reporting what he heard from residents in the town of Dresden. He traveled to the town and duly reported everything he saw and heard in carefully written letters and reports.

Two other individuals who played a significant role in Canadian human rights were vital to Hugh's cause. Ben Kayfetz, executive secretary of the Canadian Jewish Congress, provided input on the issues reported in the town. Rabbi Abraham Feinberg of Holy Blossom Temple in Toronto, the spiritual leader of the largest Jewish congregation in Canada, dedicated his life to fighting against racism and for the cause of social justice. He helped the NUA find legal help in its fight.

In building their case against discrimination, the NUA and the Joint Labour Committee gathered new information. They found that, in 1954, Dresden had more than 350 black and 1,750 white citizens. On the farms surrounding the town lived 1,000 African-Canadians and 9,000 white Canadians. The NUA also discovered that more black Dresden citizens than white fought in World War II. The only person from the area killed in the Korean War was a black man.

The NUA found that there were a few marriages between blacks and whites. Most of the black farmers were just as prosperous as their white neighbors;

however, few, if any, jobs outside of farming were available to black people.

From its discussions with Dresden citizens, the NUA heard that most white people did not want discrimination. They feared the negative publicity that came from newspaper stories portraying them as prejudiced. But at the same time, those citizens didn't want to "stick their necks out" in support of their black neighbors – they were too afraid of losing their white friends. Except for the Catholic church, the "white" churches in Dresden did not welcome blacks. If blacks showed up at a white church, they would be asked politely why they didn't attend their "own church." Those white ministers who were brave enough to support the integration of churches in Dresden did not last long in the town – they were soon driven out by the anger of its white citizens.

Clearly, the work of the NUA was not finished. But, in April 1954, the association got some really good news: the Ontario Legislature passed the Fair Accommodation Practices Act. The Act ensured that any complaint about discrimination in a public place would be followed by an investigation and conciliation. Conciliation meant that the people or groups involved would sit down and try to find a solution. If the problem still wasn't solved, the Act called for the individual or business accused of discrimination to be prosecuted.

The Act laid down relatively mild penalties. A person found guilty under the Act could be fined $50; a business could be fined twice that amount.

Finally, there could be no doubt that the businesses in Dresden that persisted in denying service to blacks were breaking the law. Surely now they would change their ways?

Defiance!

"It's a feeling I can't quite explain. Do you know that for three days afterward I get raging mad every time I see a Negro. Maybe it's like an animal who's had the smell of blood." These were the words Morley McKay used to explain to a reporter from *Maclean's* magazine how he felt when he was asked to serve black customers in his restaurant.

McKay, the owner of Kay's Café, was a balding, heavyset man, with the look of a middleweight boxer gone out of shape after retirement but still jabbing at shadows from the past. Many in the town said he was more suited to America's Deep South, where racism was rampant, than to southwestern Ontario.

It was clear that McKay was full of contradictions. He was known to be friendly to many black citizens, but only when he saw them on the street. As long as they didn't ask for sit-down service in his restaurant, he could be pleasant and even courteous. Hugh Burnett would later talk about how he'd known McKay all his life.

But Morley McKay was not prepared to bend to the new law making discrimination illegal.

The Act looked fine on paper. The penalties, while modest, at least confirmed the fact that it was against the law to discriminate. But for many people in Dresden, the law was just ink on paper. It had no real power to change their behavior.

Life went on as usual. When newspaper reporters called with questions, members of the Dresden Town Council answered, without hesitation, that there was no problem. Or they said that "the problem will solve itself."

The Fair Accommodation Practices Act came into effect on June 5, 1954. Most businesses in Dresden accepted the law and opened their doors to black people, but a few continued to discriminate. Kay's Café and Emerson's Soda Bar Restaurant, in particular, resisted the law. The NUA and the Joint Labour Committee decided to "test" the establishments. They would gather details of what happened in each restaurant when a black person tried to get served there, and then call on the Ontario government to enforce the law.

As a result of complaints from the activists, the Minister of Labour, Charles Daley, sent a factory inspector to Dresden to investigate. A long-time politician, Daley definitely was not on the side of the NUA. He felt that the Fair Accommodation Practices Act had been forced upon him. He spoke of bringing in simple policies of "education" to let people know that they were doing wrong and should behave better. The inspector Daley sent to Dresden seems to have understood that his boss was not serious about enforcing the Act.

When the inspector arrived, Dresden was quiet. The avenues of the town were dry, and dust devils swirled on St. George Street. In the cool shade of Kay's Café, the inspector talked quietly with Morley McKay.

National Archives/Getty Images

Love and Law

In February 1957, U.S. President Dwight D. Eisenhower summed up what many white people thought in those days about making laws to end discrimination. He told a reporter: "You cannot change people's hearts merely by laws."

Martin Luther King, Jr., who was to become North America's most famous civil-rights leader, had a succinct answer for the president: "A law may not make a man love me, but it can stop him from lynching me."

McKay and the inspector, it seemed, saw eye to eye. In fact, the inspector wrote in his report that there was "no evidence of discrimination in Dresden." He also told McKay openly that he could continue to discriminate against anyone he wanted to. After the visit, the Ministry of Labour told Sid Blum not to interfere in Dresden because it might "upset the town."

The NUA was not about to give up. Instead, they set about gathering evidence against the lawbreakers in an even more consistent and determined manner.

The warm spring turned into a hot summer. Southwestern Ontario is known as Canada's "banana belt," where the summers typically feature lots of cloudless days, intense sun, and cooling showers in the evening. Outside the town, in the rolling fields, clutches of crimson tomatoes caught the sun the way the shoulder patches of red-winged blackbirds reflect the light as the birds wing across the fields. Green rows of tough soybean plants hugged the deep, brown earth. Like their crops, generations of farmers had survived under the hot sun of southwestern Ontario.

Inside the town, it became a season of anger and rage. While many denied the existence of racism, others pushed for change. Almost everyone among the white population resented the fact that outsiders were taking an interest in their town. They felt that they alone were being judged unfairly, but that they were no different from any other town.

The NUA began sending black patrons to the two restaurants that continued to defy Premier Frost's law: Kay's Café and Emerson's Soda Bar Restaurant. Emerson's Restaurant was owned and operated by Matthew Emerson and his wife Anne. The Emersons, while not as excitable as McKay, were just as determined in their refusal to obey the law.

Hugh Burnett received an increasing number of anonymous hate letters and calls. And, while at one time he could hire on as many as five workers for his carpentry business, now he was beginning to lose clients. People were refusing to hire him. He went more than $3,000 in debt.

Even worse, there were more death threats, which he was starting to take seriously. To protect his family, he purchased a handgun for protection.

A story in the *Toronto Telegram* headlined "Dresden Negro Warned, Gets Gun for Safety," told how Hugh came to arm himself. The reporter went on, writing that

. . . in Dresden, the restaurant proprietors who refused to serve "black men" refused to comment on the situation. Senior civil officials were "not at home to the press." And some ordinary citizens said "This has nothing to do with anybody who lives outside Dresden. It's our affair and we'll handle it our way."

Making the Papers

Not everyone was convinced that Dresden should be left to solve its problems on its own. The *Toronto Telegram* newspaper, in particular, began a campaign of publishing hard-hitting, emotional articles about the situation. *Telegram* reporter Gordon Donaldson wrote pieces as events unfolded. Donaldson was an inspiration to others in the civil-rights community, a white reporter who was determined to expose discrimination until something was done to end it. Another Toronto reporter, the *Toronto Star*'s Pat McNenly, would also visit Dresden and contribute stories about the town.

In June 1954, the *Toronto Telegram* ran a photograph of a black Chatham mailman, Richard Henderson. Henderson, his wife and two children, and Hugh Burnett were refused service at Kay's Café, even though they were the only customers in the restaurant. A waitress told them that the restaurant staff was "too busy to serve them." A headline under the photo announced "'We sat there and were ignored.'"

Later in the month, two African-Canadian couples, Mr. and Mrs. Shadd and Mr. and Mrs. Robbins, tried to get served at Kay's Café at eight forty-five in the evening. They were told to go to Martin's Dairy Bar instead. When they couldn't contact the police chief, they called Hugh. He joined them, and together they went back into Kay's Café. More than five groups of people, all white, came in and were served while Hugh and his companions waited. About twenty-five minutes later, an angry Morley McKay appeared and confronted them.

In a sworn statement, Hugh told of the conversation with McKay:

Mr. Morley McKay came in the rear door and walked over to me and said, 'Hugh, you might as well get your boys out because I am not going to serve them.' I asked why and he said 'That is my business.' Then he went by the table that had the party of colored people and told them in answer to their request for service that he would not serve them. At 9:30 I phoned the police again and the Chief told me the Crown Attorney said not to go in unless there was trouble. We all left then and Mr. Shadd, Mr. Robbins, and myself went to the police station to make a report to them.

No one else in the café stood up for the group. Clearly, when the townspeople said they would handle things in their own way, what they meant was that they would not handle things at all.

The NUA and the activists from Toronto continued to demand that the government take action. At the same time, they made arrangements for more blacks and whites to continue visiting the two restaurants.

The goal was simple: watch, listen, and observe. Would black patrons be served? The white testers and observers would keep track of what happened and help prove that whites were being given preferential treatment. These observations would serve as a public record, in the event the NUA and the Joint Labour Committee had to take the offending restaurant owners to court.

Like McKay and the Emersons, others in town were having a hard time adjusting to the new law. In July, Hugh, accompanied by Sid Blum, went into Ford's Barber Shop and asked for a shave. The proprietor, James Ford, was sitting with a few of the local folks. "Now you *know* you're not going to get a shave here," Ford told Hugh. When told that the law required him to provide service, Ford replied, "The hell with you and the law too!"

While the police said that they were sympathetic to the National Unity Association, they and A. Douglas Bell, the Crown attorney in charge of the local legal department, did little to help. The police, under the direction of Chief Alvin Watson, investigated and provided some protection for Hugh, but it amounted to only an hourly drive by his house. No protection was offered to other members of the Association. And though the police worked to find the person who wrote the letters threatening Hugh, they came up with no leads.

The NUA wrote to the government, complaining of the situation. In a letter to Clifford Magone at the Department of Justice, Hugh wrote of an "anonymous letter threatening my life," the verbal threats because of the group's efforts to eliminate racial discrimination in Dresden, and a rumor that his house might be burned down. Fortunately for Hugh, the threats were empty.

The testing continued. In the fall, two black Torontonians, Julian Brooks and Gladys Grizzle, entered Kay's Café and also visited two other restaurants, Emerson's Restaurant and Martin's Dairy Bar. The *Toronto Telegram*'s Gordon Donaldson recorded what happened at Kay's for his readers.

The café was typical for the times, with a linoleum floor and fixtures of polished stainless steel. A soda bar and booths ran along the side walls. Food was passed from the kitchen through a hole about the size of a small television screen in the wall opposite the front door. Brooks and Grizzle sat down at a booth. The menu featured the specials of the day, and the smell of good, home-cooked food drifted in from the kitchen.

The pair sat and waited. And waited. They glanced out the window and saw Dresden residents walking, cycling, or driving by the restaurant. The lone waitress served white customers or kept herself busy behind the soda bar. Six times the waitress walked past the couple and never served them. Then, finally, they asked her if they were not being served because of their color. She told them yes, that "it was a policy" that they not be served.

Morley McKay stayed behind the scenes, barely visible through the small hole in the wall, preparing food. When Brooks asked to speak with the manager, the waitress went to the back to talk to McKay, then came back and ignored them. When asked again why she wouldn't serve them, she told them that McKay said she didn't have to give a reason. All the time this was happening, no other customer in the restaurant said or did anything. They simply sat and watched.

After the testers left, they made notes of what happened. At the second restaurant, Martin's Dairy Bar, Brooks and Grizzle were served. The owner told Donaldson afterwards that he was glad to have the new law in place, because it meant he could do more business by serving black customers. But at the third restaurant, Emerson's Soda Bar Restaurant, Anne Emerson refused to serve them. She gave quick and friendly service to Donaldson, but she ignored the black couple. When the pair asked for service, Emerson sat in the kitchen and would not come out. Finally Brooks and Grizzle left.

Donaldson wrote in a newspaper story that he was "ashamed and embarrassed as I saw the way they were treated. And I shared their helpless indignation as we discovered the police could do nothing about it."

Published in a big Toronto newspaper, Donaldson's story made an impact. People far from Dresden were watching what was happening. For folks in the town, it served notice: "No – this town will not be ignored. We're here for the duration."

The tests of Kay's Café and Emerson's Soda Bar Restaurant were repeated several times. Each time the testers kept notes of how they were treated.

By the time the first phase of testing was over, eight complaints had been filed with the Ontario government under the Fair Accommodation Practices Act. The government called for a hearing – evidence would be presented and an attempt would be made to find the truth of what happened.

That hearing took place in September 1954. The judge, William F. Schwenger, listened to Hugh Burnett and four others from the black community. They told him that Morley McKay had refused them service. Lyle Talbot, another member of the black community, said he and other blacks were turned away from Emerson's Soda Bar Restaurant. At the hearing, Morley McKay admitted to the discrimination, saying, "I have the right to break the law to protect my business. *I have a right to.* My customers have told me if we serve Negroes, they won't come in."

The *Toronto Telegram* followed the hearing with a story that carried the headline "Race Law Fails, Negroes Insulted." Gordon Donaldson wrote, "the men and women responsible for Dresden's reputation as the stronghold of color prejudice in Canada are ignoring the law. And, as it now stands, the law gives a Negro no effective legal redress from the insults that are heaped upon him."

Judge Schwenger agreed. He wrote in his report that Morley McKay should be charged under the Act and sent to trial for breaking the law. Schwenger handed in his report to the Labour Ministry and, for a time, nothing more was heard. In fact, Labour Minister Charles Daley took the report and hid it from the public. He refused to let the public know what Schwenger had said.

But even this was not enough to stop the NUA and the Toronto Labour Committee.

Sid Blum, members of the NUA, and Toronto activist Bromley Armstrong visited Kay's Café three more times. Bromley Armstrong belonged to the United Autoworkers Union and served on the Joint Labour Committee's board of directors. A determined fighter in his mid-twenties, Armstrong was a rough-and-ready activist with a never-say-die attitude. He worked for a large manufacturing company called Massey Harris, and was a union representative who fought for the rights of minorities in the workplace. Armstrong had already been active in tests like this in other places, including the Mercury Athletic Club in Toronto, where the previous year he had been told to leave and was escorted out.

In the September test, Armstrong was the only black customer and, although others were served, Blum, Armstrong, and their group were not. When they entered the café, the waitress went to the back of the restaurant. Soon after, a kitchen worker wearing a white apron went to the front of the restaurant, shut the blinds, locked the door, and turned out some of the lights. The group waited twenty minutes for service that never came. Twice in early October the group was again refused service.

In late October 1954, the Joint Labour Committee sent two more people into town. As with Julian Brooks and Gladys Grizzle, the committee decided that the best way to test the treatment of restaurant patrons was with people who would not be as well-known as those living in or around Dresden. It was felt that if visitors from Toronto went into Kay's Café, they would get the evidence the activists needed to have McKay charged under the law. Also, the discrimination could not be misinterpreted as simply a reaction to known "troublemakers" from inside the town.

The "outsiders" who came to Dresden were seasoned activists who had been fighting for equal rights for years. Among them were Bromley Armstrong, who had visited the town a few weeks earlier, and Ruth Lor.

Shortly after graduating in 1954, Ruth Lor decided to join the Toronto Joint Labour Committee on Human Rights after walking into its office, and "enquiring about the work of that labour organization which I had heard was the only action group in its field in Ontario."
Courtesy of Ruth Lor Malloy

A Canadian of Chinese descent, Ruth Lor was determined to help prove that McKay was practicing bigotry in his everyday dealings with Dresden's black community. She was twenty-two years old and a recent graduate of the University of Toronto, where she had been the secretary of the University of Toronto Student Christian Movement. Lor had already taken part in civil-rights actions in the American capital of Washington, D.C.

Lor and Armstrong had worked together before, testing the discriminatory practices of apartment-building owners in Toronto. They had a good rapport and a sense of how to approach difficult situations together.

They entered the restaurant and sat down. Also in the restaurant were reporters from the Toronto newspapers, as well as Sid Blum. Everyone else was served but, as with the African-Canadians who had come before them, Armstrong and Lor were left waiting for service.

Eventually, Bromley Armstrong got up from the table to see if he could get service. He went to the back of the restaurant and peered through the service window. In a small kitchen lit by a bare bulb, Morley McKay was striking a meat cleaver against a chopping block – even though there was no meat on it. McKay glanced at Armstrong, his eyes red with anger. When Armstrong asked for service, the chopping became louder and stronger. McKay's face burned with rage. Armstrong decided that he had better return to his seat. It was obvious that McKay was getting angrier by the second, and Armstrong was worried that McKay might throw the cleaver at him.

A few minutes later, the group left the restaurant. When they went to Emerson's Soda Bar Restaurant, the door was already locked, even though it was still early in the afternoon. They figured that the Emersons had seen them coming, or that McKay had called to let them know the group was on its way.

The incidents received national coverage.

In a story that appeared on October 30, 1954, *Toronto Star* reporter Pat McNenly wrote,

Premier Frost's much publicized anti-discrimination legislation has failed in five months to dent this historic town's rigid color bar. Today some 300 Negroes, descendants of U.S. slaves who fled to freedom to the town made famous by Uncle Tom, are still denied meals and haircuts in most of the town's establishments and are not wanted in service clubs, pool rooms and most churches. Two young Torontonians found yesterday that some Dresden restaurant operators have little regard for the Frost government's Fair Accommodation Practices act which makes it a statutory offence to discriminate in public places on grounds of 'race, creed, color, nationality, ancestry (or) place of origin.'

The Trials of Morley McKay

On Tuesday, November 2, 1954, the *Toronto Daily Star* carried a story with a front-page headline in big letters: "FROST SENDS DRESDEN ULTIMATUM." The article reported that the premier would insist upon the prosecution of anyone who continued to defy the Fair Accommodation Practices Act.

A few days after this story was printed, more testing took place. On November 7, Joseph Hanson (a farmer and one of the founders of the NUA) and his sister, Mrs. Bernard Carter (wife of NUA co-founder Bernie Carter), went to Emerson's Restaurant. When they sat down, Anne Emerson went into the kitchen and sent out a young boy to lock the front door, preventing other customers from coming in. Mrs. Carter went to the kitchen to ask for service. She asked for a bottle of soda and was told, "We have no pop."

Then Anne Emerson became angrier and shouted, "Stay away from the kitchen and stay at the front of the restaurant!" Shortly after, Mrs. Carter filed a complaint.

Labour Minister Daley, under pressure from Premier Frost, couldn't keep ignoring such defiance of the law. He announced that the government would take McKay, along with Anne Emerson and her husband, Matthew, to court for their refusal to provide service to black patrons. Soon the leaders of the National Unity Association, along with the members of the Toronto Joint Labour Committee, found themselves in court, along with the accused and their

lawyers, taking part in the proceedings that resulted from years of pushing
for change.

The trial took place on December 8, 1954, in Chatham, Ontario. The
defense said the complaint was a "frame-up" of McKay and Emerson that was
designed to make them look bad. The defense lawyer, W.A. Donohue, called
the Fair Accommodation Practices Act illegal and unworkable. "It imposes an
impossible task on the prosecution . . . the Crown has to prove the state of mind
of the accused," said Donohue. He also said that, because it was criminal law, it
should be the responsibility of the federal government, not the province of
Ontario. The Crown attorney, A.D. Bell, countered that the rights of citizens to
equal treatment was a matter for the province and should be handled by the
province, not the federal government.

McKay tried to evade many of the questions he was asked by Mr. Bell. He
also tried to defend himself by saying that if he served black customers, he
would lose his white customers.

And Anne Emerson? Some in the courtroom said she was so nervous that
her makeup began to run, drawing lines of perspiration down the white powder
she had applied to her face that morning.

The judge, Ivan B. Craig, reserved his decision, saying that it would be
"some time" before the judgment would be made, either for or against
the defendants.

On January 14, 1955, McKay and Emerson were found guilty. Judge Craig
convicted them of breaking the anti-discrimination law as laid out in the Fair
Accommodation Practices Act, and fined them $50 plus the court costs. For
Morley McKay, this worked out to $135.40, and for Anne Emerson, $74.18.
If they didn't pay their fines, they would have to spend thirty days in jail.

In his decision, the judge said it was clear that the customers had been
refused because they were "colored members of the Negro race" and that there
was no other reasonable conclusion for him to reach. He also confirmed that
the Fair Accommodation Practices Act was a piece of legislation that should be
delivered by the province, not by the federal government.

After the decision, Hugh Burnett told the *London Free Press* that the
National Unity Association really just wanted to bring the matter to a close:

Our ultimate aim is not causing the shop owners to pay fines but to secure fair treatment for our group. We invite white leaders and shop owners to sit around the table with us and settle our problems once and for all.

But McKay and the Emersons decided to appeal the decision. This meant another judge would review it. That judge turned out to be County Court judge Henry E. Grosch.

Judge Grosch had a reputation of being against fair practices in the town. In fact, a newspaper reporter managed to dig up information showing that Grosch was involved in a land deal with a requirement that, according to official records, his property

. . . shall never be occupied or used in any manner whatsoever by any person of the Jewish, Hebrew, Semitic, Negro or coloured race or blood, it being the intention and purpose of the Grantor, to restrict the owner-ship, use, occupation and enjoyment of the said recreational development, including the lands and premises herein described, to persons of the white or Caucasian race not excluded by this clause.

So it didn't come as a surprise to the activists when, by the end of August 1955, Judge Grosch had overturned Judge Craig's decision, saying that there was no clear evidence of racial discrimination, and that service had not been refused, only "postponed" for personal reasons. Grosch said the testers were there to "provoke" Morley McKay, and that it was fair for McKay to not want to become involved with the NUA's attempts to "test" the restaurant's service. He even suggested that "there quite possibly could also be reasons other than color if service was in fact denied."

This outraged the NUA, the Joint Labour Committee, and the media. When news of the decision reached the Ontario Legislature and landed on the desk of Premier Leslie Frost, the premier was angry, too – after all, Frost had personally directed the creation of the Fair Accommodation Practices Act, and he expected judges to enforce it.

The Emersons later decided to give up their fight, but Morley McKay was pleased with his victory. In November 1955, the Toronto Labour Committee sent two black university students, Jake Alleyne and Percy Bruce, to Kay's Café. A white student, Robert Van Alstyne, entered the restaurant after them. Van Alstyne was served while the black students waited for service that never came. The white student made careful notes about the treatment of Alleyne and Bruce in preparation for another court case.

Early the next year, Morley McKay was charged again with violating the Fair Accommodation Practices Act by refusing to serve the two university students. A delegation to Premier Frost received assurances that Frost was confident the charge would result in a conviction. McKay went back to court, and his lawyer argued that McKay was not responsible for denying service. The lawyer also said that the observer in the café, the white university student, was just a "spy" sent from Toronto.

Those arguments were rejected, and in February 1956 Morley McKay was found guilty. He was fined $50 on each of two counts against him, plus the court costs. The court costs were very high – more than $600. McKay appealed again. The judge who heard the case offered to excuse McKay from having to pay the court costs. McKay's lawyer, however, said he wanted to "go down fighting" – he wanted to let people know he didn't like the new law and wanted to uphold the unfair principles of segregation. McKay was going to take the case to the Supreme Court of Ontario. But before the case got to court, he decided to give it up. Perhaps he finally realized that he just couldn't win.

Justice?

"He couldn't get a job. He was a carpenter, they would not give him any work, and they did everything to destroy him till he died." This is what Bromley Armstrong said about Hugh Burnett's life after the events described in this book.

Justice finally came to Dresden on November 16, 1956, when a group from the National Unity Association went into Kay's Café and Morley McKay served them.

A story written by the Canadian Press news service on December 25, 1956, told of a

> . . . happy story about the town where the original Uncle Tom was buried. It's told by two Negroes who emerged smiling from a restaurant where they have always been rebuffed. They said they were served as would be anyone else.

Clearly, times had changed, and the citizens of Dresden had the law on their side. In defeat, the likes of Morley McKay, Anne Emerson, and James Ford faded into the life of the town, melting into the fabric of Dresden's history.

But many attitudes didn't change. In Dresden, the goal of changing behavior was achieved when the courts upheld the Fair Accommodation Practices Act. But it didn't necessarily mean that people's attitudes improved. So while justice had been served in the town, the leader of the National Unity Association was never able to fully enjoy it. Because of the long fight, Hugh Burnett's business had suffered. He lost clients and even some of his friends. People who were angry about the court decision refused to give him any work. They turned away from him on the street. When Hugh visited former clients, they said there was nothing they could do for him.

Despite, or maybe because of, his efforts to bring justice to Dresden, by the late 1950s Hugh Burnett had to leave his hometown.
Courtesy of the Burnett family

Hugh Burnett was forced to leave Dresden, looking for work. He moved to London, Ontario, in 1957. Over the next thirty years he worked for a number of companies and continued to run his own carpentry business. The remainder of his life was lived out of the public eye. He died in 1991. His body was cremated and his ashes buried in a plot he shares with his parents in the Dresden Cemetery.

Morley McKay would continue to operate his restaurant for several more years. On a cold day in January 1972, McKay, the man who came to symbolize the anger and resentment of Dresden's white community, died. He was buried in the Dresden Cemetery, not far from Hugh Burnett.

In the capital of Toronto, Premier Leslie Frost led the province of Ontario into a new age, as Canada began to emerge as a significant leader in the world. In addition to championing human rights, he laid the groundwork for advances in education and health, and encouraged growth in private industry. In 1961, he retired from public office. Far to the east of Dresden, in the town of Lindsay, Ontario, the man who brought the issue of fairness into the province's political forum and made it into law lies in his family grave, where he was buried in 1973. The small-minded small-town values that folks in Dresden spoke of so often, the "leave-us-alone" attitudes that tried to defeat fairness in the town, were struck down by a small-town premier whose political life was based on his own set of pragmatic and visionary values.

For the National Unity Association, there was recognition for its work from human-rights organizations. The NUA would continue to support other challenges to equal treatment, such as workplace discrimination and the refusal to rent apartments on the basis of skin color. But its work was winding down. As time went by, the group slowly disbanded. By the early 1970s, it was officially no longer an association. In 1973, the Ontario Human Rights Commission held a dinner for the group, and each member was given a Certificate of Merit.

And the other founders of the National Unity Association? A part of the community – like the rich earth and the green crops that surrounded Dresden, like the history that began with lumber barons and a brave black man named Josiah Henson – they stayed on. They were hardy souls who carried within them the quiet knowledge that they had done the right thing, and they passed their wisdom on to the next generation. They would come to rest in the pages of Dresden's history, their energy, determination, and action becoming a part of the collective memory of a town, a province, and a country.

The work of the National Unity Association and the Joint Labour Committee created an important precedent, helping set the stage for the establishment of the Ontario Human Rights Commission. Daniel G. Hill – husband of Donna Hill, the former secretary of the Joint Labour Committee – was the Commission's first chair.

The Commission was established in 1961, and continues to be responsible for Ontario's Human Rights Code. Created in 1962, the Human Rights Code protects Ontario citizens from discrimination in employment, accommodation, goods, services, and facilities, as well as in membership in associations and unions. The Ontario Human Rights Commission continues to investigate all cases of discrimination against Ontario's citizens.

The other civil-rights groups that rallied to Dresden's cause continued their work: challenging government to enact better policies for allowing the immigration of non-whites to Canada; keeping an eye on police forces and their treatment of minorities; and pushing for fairness in employment and accommodation.

Fifty years later, the activists remember this dramatic time. Donna Hill said it was the most exciting and challenging time of her new life in Canada. For Ruth Lor, it was a chance to really take action against racism, and it just made sense to her to be a part of that history. Alvin Ladd, the last surviving founder of the NUA, said it was justice that was a long time coming.

Bromley Armstrong, now retired, worked in Dresden and other places to challenge discriminatory attitudes in the 1950s. John Cooper

For Bromley Armstrong, the significance was driven home when the National Film Board went to Dresden to make a film, *Journey to Justice*. An eighty-seven-year-old black man saw the cameras, recognized Armstrong and Ruth Lor (who was with him) and approached and hugged them both. With tears in his eyes, he said that as a child he couldn't buy an ice cream cone anywhere in the town. He spoke of his father and his grandfather being refused service everywhere, and how generations of blacks grew so used to the words "No Service." Armstrong and Lor took the old man to lunch, on the very street where it all took place, moving freely along the avenue that once screamed a silent and resounding "NO" to so many of Dresden's citizens.

Timeline: The Civil-Rights Movement

Slavery, Harriet Tubman said, was "the next thing to hell." But even after slavery was abolished, black people in both the U.S. and Canada continued to endure personal insults, economic disadvantages, and the constant threat of physical violence. White people were in charge of just about everything, including big corporations, professions like medicine and law, and government. Jim Crow laws determined how black people lived their lives and set a limit on what they could hope to achieve. White people weren't about to change the system. It was up to black people to shake things up.

And they did. Hugh Burnett was not alone. At the same time that he and the NUA were striking a blow against prejudice in Dresden, a great movement was beginning in the southern U.S. The history of this movement includes moments of triumph, terrible setbacks, legal progress, and bloody tragedy. The story is not over yet. This timeline marks some of the significant incidents in the history of the civil-rights movement in the years during and after Hugh Burnett's struggle against racism in his own small town.

1941	Under pressure from the National Association for the Advancement of Colored People (NAACP) and the Congress on Racial Equality (CORE), the U.S. President's Committee on Fair Employment Practices prohibits discrimination in the workplace.
1943-45	U.S. involvement in World War II. American factories are working at maximum capacity to meet the demands of the war. Two million African-Americans get jobs in defense-related industries. The Army, needing more soldiers, integrates the officer training program.

1947

Publication of *To Secure These Rights: The Report of the President's Committee on Civil Rights.* The committee, appointed by U.S. President Truman, drew attention to the harsh effects of discrimination on the black community.

1950

June 5: U.S. Supreme Court hands down three important judgments. In *Henderson v. U.S.* the court holds that segregation on railway dining cars is illegal. In *McLaurin v. Oklahoma State Regents* it rules that a black student cannot be kept physically apart from white students. And in *Sweatt v. Painter* it orders the University of Texas to admit a black student, Herman Sweatt, to the law school, on the grounds that the state has not provided an equal education for him.

1954

May 17: U.S. Supreme Court rules in *Brown v. Board of Education of Topeka* that all races are entitled to equal treatment under the law. Chief Justice Earl Warren writes that segregation of children in schools "solely because of their race generates a feeling of inferiority as to their status in the community that may affect their hearts and minds in a way unlikely ever to be undone."

1955

In a judgment known as Brown II, the U.S. Supreme Court refuses to set a timetable for school desegregation. The court says only that the ruling should be implemented "with all deliberate speed." This gives southern states an excuse to move slowly.

December 1: Rosa Parks refuses to give up her seat on the bus to a white person in Montgomery, Alabama.

Don Cravens/Time Life Pictures/Getty Images

The Montgomery Bus Boycott

Rosa Parks (above, center) was a 42-year-old seamstress in Montgomery, Alabama. On a December evening, when she was returning home from her job in a department store, she was asked by a bus driver to give up her seat to a white man. This was the law in Montgomery. Rosa Parks refused to obey it.

Most people who rode the buses in Montgomery were black. The black people of the city got together and decided that they would not ride the buses until the city changed the law and ended the discrimination. The boycott lasted for a year. It was organized partly by the NAACP and partly by the local churches. The Reverend Martin Luther King, Jr., pastor of Dexter Avenue Baptist Church in Montgomery, first came to national attention as a leader and spokesperson for the boycott. His house was bombed and he and his followers were harassed by police. But they won in the end. In December 1956, the U.S. Supreme Court ruled that segregation on buses was illegal.

1957   Nine black students in Little Rock, Arkansas, attempt to start classes at the segregated (white) Central High School.

A.Y. Owen/Time Life Pictures/Getty Images

Confrontation in Little Rock

The Supreme Court had declared that the segregation of races in public schools was illegal. Although the southern states were ordered to open all schools to blacks, in many cases they acted very slowly to do what they were told.

The NAACP encouraged nine students in Little Rock, Arkansas, simply to show up at an all-white school – Central High School – when school started in September 1957. The governor of the state, Orville Faubus, responded by ordering the National Guard to surround the school. Hundreds of white people followed the nine black children, shouting and even spitting at them. The National Guard let white children into the school, but stopped the black children. The state was defying the federal government. President Dwight Eisenhower finally sent in federal troops to end the standoff. The incident showed blacks once again that they would have to take action to get governments to enforce the law.

1957

U.S. Congress passes the first civil-rights bill since just after the Civil War. The bill guarantees all Americans the right to vote in federal elections.

Martin Luther King helps establish the Southern Christian Leadership Conference (SCLC) to help make church organizations a part of the civil-rights movement.

1960

February 1: Four freshmen from all-black A&T College sit down at a downtown lunch counter in Greensboro, North Carolina. The staff refuses to serve them.

The Sit-in Campaign

The lunch-counter protest in Greensboro immediately inspired thousands of other black students take similar action. Within two weeks, sit-ins spread to fifteen cities in five southern states. The following year, an estimated 50,000 people took part in some kind of demonstration to end segregation. Thousands of demonstrators spent time in jail for their participation. But the protests worked. By the end of 1961, several hundred lunch counters were desegregated in cities across the country.

1961

"Freedom Rides" organized by CORE send volunteers across the U.S. to ride on segregated trains and buses, and make the federal government enforce the law.

1963

April 12: Martin Luther King and other movement leaders organize a march in Birmingham, Alabama, which King calls America's "worst big city" for racism. They are met by the city's Public Safety Commissioner, who turns police dogs on the protesters.

1963

August 28: A quarter-million people participate in the March on Washington.

September 10: A bomb destroys the 16th Street Baptist Church in Birmingham during a Bible-study class. Fourteen black children are injured and four are killed.

AFP/Getty Images

The Dream

In August 1963, Martin Luther King gave what many people consider to be his most memorable speech from the steps of the Lincoln Memorial in Washington, D.C. Hundreds of people were there with him. Millions more watched him on TV. The speech was famous for its inspiring refrain – "I have a dream" – and its rousing concluding quotation from an

African-American spiritual: "Free at last, free at last; thank God Almighty, we are free at last."

King's vision was still a dream in 1963. There would be many more marches, protests, sit-ins, and demonstrations. The summer of 1964 became famous as Freedom Summer, when hundreds of young people headed for the southern states where Jim Crow laws still governed relations between the races. Three youths who had volunteered to help register black voters were murdered in Mississippi. Many others suffered abuse, beatings, and jail. The movement grew stronger, but the violence made the fight more bitter.

In March 1968, King was shot dead by an assassin in Memphis, Tennessee. There had always been other leaders, and they now took King's place. New organizations appeared on the scene, and a new sense of militancy gave energy to the movement.

It was people like Hugh Burnett who gave the civil-rights movement its start. One man, standing up for what he believed to be right, made a small difference. But put together with a dozen men and women – and then a hundred, and then thousands – the course of history was changed.

Acknowledgments

T he author would like to acknowledge the following for their assistance and guidance, and in several cases for the opportunity to interview them personally or gain access to their written or visual materials, during the time it took to research and write this book: Spencer Alexander (of the Buxton National Historic Site and Museum), who has been a great help in sourcing information on Dresden; Bromley Armstrong (and his autobiography, *Bromley: Tireless Champion for Just Causes*); Lorraine Brown-Johnston; Beatrice Burnett; Cecil Burnett; Cheryl Burnett; Gordon Burnette; Gordon Donaldson's articles in the *Toronto Telegram*; Dr. Arlington Dungy; Hilda Dungy (author of *Planted By The Waters*); Mayor Diane Gagner, Municipality of Chatham-Kent; Roger M. Graham's book *Old Man Ontario: Leslie M. Frost*; Stanley G. Grizzle; Donna Hill; Lawrence Hill; Ross Lambertson; Ruth Lor Malloy; Pat McNenly (and his articles in the *Toronto Star*); Roger McTair (director of the National Film Board production *Journey to Justice*); Sinclair Shadd; Don Spearman's book *Landmarks from the Past*; Professor James Walker; staff at the National Archives of Canada; and the reference staff at the Chatham Public Library, the Dresden Branch of the Chatham-Kent Public Library, and the Whitby Public Library.

My thanks also to editor Kat Mototsune for her insightful comments and concise editing, and to Tundra Publisher Kathy Lowinger for her continued support and enthusiasm in bringing this story to a young audience.

Suggested Reading

Harriet's Daughter, by Marlene Nourbese Philip; published by The Women's Press.

I Came As A Stranger, by Bryan Prince; published by Tundra Books.

Leading The Way, by Rosemary Sadlier; published by Umbrella Press.

Mary Ann Shadd, by Rosemary Sadlier; published by Umbrella Press.

Rapid Ray: The Story of Ray Lewis, by John Cooper; published by Tundra Books.

Steel Drums and Ice Skates, by Dirk McLean; published by Douglas and McIntyre Ltd.

The Black Canadians: Their History and Their Contributions, by Velma Carter and Levero Carter Reidmore; published by Books Inc.

Trials and Triumphs: The Story of African-Canadians, by Lawrence Hill; published by Umbrella Press.